# GO HARD
## FITNESS JOURNAL

### NO GOAL WAS MET WITHOUT A LITTLE SWEAT

## ACTIVINOTES

**Activinotes**

DAILY JOURNALS, PLANNERS, NOTEBOOKS AND OTHER BLANK BOOKS

DAY: _____

NAME: _____

| | | DESCRIPTION | QTY | PROTEINS | VEGGIES | FRUITS & NUTS | FATS |
|---|---|---|---|---|---|---|---|
| **BREAKFAST** | | | | | | | |
| | | | | | | | |
| TIME | | | | | | | |
| | | | | | | | |
| TOTAL | | | | | | | |

| | | DESCRIPTION | QTY | PROTEINS | VEGGIES | FRUITS & NUTS | FATS |
|---|---|---|---|---|---|---|---|
| **LUNCH** | | | | | | | |
| | | | | | | | |
| TIME | | | | | | | |
| | | | | | | | |
| TOTAL | | | | | | | |

| | | DESCRIPTION | QTY | PROTEINS | VEGGIES | FRUITS & NUTS | FATS |
|---|---|---|---|---|---|---|---|
| **DINNER** | | | | | | | |
| | | | | | | | |
| TIME | | | | | | | |
| | | | | | | | |
| TOTAL | | | | | | | |

| | |
|---|---|
| **SNACKS** | |
| TIME | |
| | |

|  | CORE BODY | UPPER BODY | LOWER BODY |
|---|---|---|---|
| EXERCISES | | | |
| SETS | | | |
| REPS | | | |
| WEIGHTS | | | |
| REST TIME | | | |

|  | WARM UP | COOL DOWN |
|---|---|---|
| ACTIVITY | | |
| SETS | | |
| REPS | | |
| TIME | | |
| DIST | | |
| INTENSITY | | |

GOALS: _____

_____

_____

_____

_____

_____

_____

_____

_____

DAY: _____

NAME: _____

| | | DESCRIPTION | QTY | PROTEINS | VEGGIES | FRUITS & NUTS | FATS |
|---|---|---|---|---|---|---|---|
| **BREAKFAST** | | | | | | | |
| | | | | | | | |
| TIME | | | | | | | |
| | | | | | | | |
| TOTAL | | | | | | | |

| | | | | | | | |
|---|---|---|---|---|---|---|---|
| LUNCH | | | | | | | |
| | | | | | | | |
| TIME | | | | | | | |
| | | | | | | | |
| TOTAL | | | | | | | |

| | | | | | | | |
|---|---|---|---|---|---|---|---|
| DINNER | | | | | | | |
| | | | | | | | |
| TIME | | | | | | | |
| | | | | | | | |
| TOTAL | | | | | | | |

| | |
|---|---|
| SNACKS | |
| | |
| TIME | |
| | |

|  | CORE BODY | UPPER BODY | LOWER BODY |
|---|---|---|---|
| EXERCISES | | | |
| SETS | | | |
| REPS | | | |
| WEIGHTS | | | |
| REST TIME | | | |

|  | WARM UP | COOL DOWN |
|---|---|---|
| ACTIVITY | | |
| SETS | | |
| REPS | | |
| TIME | | |
| DIST | | |
| INTENSITY | | |

GOALS: _____

_____

_____

_____

_____

_____

_____

_____

DAY: _____

NAME: _____

| | DESCRIPTION | QTY | PROTEINS | VEGGIES | FRUITS & NUTS | FATS |
|---|---|---|---|---|---|---|
| **BREAKFAST** TIME | | | | | | |
| TOTAL | | | | | | |

| | DESCRIPTION | QTY | PROTEINS | VEGGIES | FRUITS & NUTS | FATS |
|---|---|---|---|---|---|---|
| LUNCH TIME | | | | | | |
| TOTAL | | | | | | |

| | DESCRIPTION | QTY | PROTEINS | VEGGIES | FRUITS & NUTS | FATS |
|---|---|---|---|---|---|---|
| DINNER TIME | | | | | | |
| TOTAL | | | | | | |

| SNACKS TIME | |
|---|---|

|  | CORE BODY | UPPER BODY | LOWER BODY |
|---|---|---|---|
| EXERCISES |  |  |  |
| SETS |  |  |  |
| REPS |  |  |  |
| WEIGHTS |  |  |  |
| REST TIME |  |  |  |

|  | WARM UP | COOL DOWN |
|---|---|---|
| ACTIVITY |  |  |
| SETS |  |  |
| REPS |  |  |
| TIME |  |  |
| DIST |  |  |
| INTENSITY |  |  |

GOALS: _____

_____

_____

_____

_____

_____

_____

_____

DAY: _____

NAME: _____

| | | DESCRIPTION | QTY | PROTEINS | VEGGIES | FRUITS & NUTS | FATS |
|---|---|---|---|---|---|---|---|
| BREAKFAST | TIME | | | | | | |
| | | | | | | | |
| | TOTAL | | | | | | |
| LUNCH | TIME | | | | | | |
| | | | | | | | |
| | TOTAL | | | | | | |
| DINNER | TIME | | | | | | |
| | | | | | | | |
| | TOTAL | | | | | | |
| SNACKS | TIME | | | | | | |

|  | CORE BODY | UPPER BODY | LOWER BODY |
|---|---|---|---|
| EXERCISES |  |  |  |
| SETS |  |  |  |
| REPS |  |  |  |
| WEIGHTS |  |  |  |
| REST TIME |  |  |  |

|  | WARM UP | COOL DOWN |
|---|---|---|
| ACTIVITY |  |  |
| SETS |  |  |
| REPS |  |  |
| TIME |  |  |
| DIST |  |  |
| INTENSITY |  |  |

GOALS: _____

_____

_____

_____

_____

_____

_____

_____

_____

DAY: _____

NAME: _____

| | DESCRIPTION | QTY | PROTEINS | VEGGIES | FRUITS & NUTS | FATS |
|---|---|---|---|---|---|---|
| **BREAKFAST** <br><br> TIME <br> ☐ | | | | | | |
| TOTAL | | | | | | |

| | DESCRIPTION | QTY | PROTEINS | VEGGIES | FRUITS & NUTS | FATS |
|---|---|---|---|---|---|---|
| **LUNCH** <br><br> TIME <br> ☐ | | | | | | |
| TOTAL | | | | | | |

| | DESCRIPTION | QTY | PROTEINS | VEGGIES | FRUITS & NUTS | FATS |
|---|---|---|---|---|---|---|
| **DINNER** <br><br> TIME <br> ☐ | | | | | | |
| TOTAL | | | | | | |

| | |
|---|---|
| **SNACKS** <br><br> TIME <br> ☐ | |

|  | CORE BODY | UPPER BODY | LOWER BODY |
|---|---|---|---|
| EXERCISES |  |  |  |
| SETS |  |  |  |
| REPS |  |  |  |
| WEIGHTS |  |  |  |
| REST TIME |  |  |  |

|  | WARM UP | COOL DOWN |
|---|---|---|
| ACTIVITY |  |  |
| SETS |  |  |
| REPS |  |  |
| TIME |  |  |
| DIST |  |  |
| INTENSITY |  |  |

GOALS: _____

_____

_____

_____

_____

_____

_____

_____

_____

DAY: _____

NAME: _____

| | | DESCRIPTION | QTY | PROTEINS | VEGGIES | FRUITS & NUTS | FATS |
|---|---|---|---|---|---|---|---|
| **BREAKFAST** | | | | | | | |
| TIME | | | | | | | |
| | | | | | | | |
| TOTAL | | | | | | | |

| | | | | | | | |
|---|---|---|---|---|---|---|---|
| **LUNCH** | | | | | | | |
| TIME | | | | | | | |
| | | | | | | | |
| TOTAL | | | | | | | |

| | | | | | | | |
|---|---|---|---|---|---|---|---|
| **DINNER** | | | | | | | |
| TIME | | | | | | | |
| | | | | | | | |
| TOTAL | | | | | | | |

| | |
|---|---|
| **SNACKS** | |
| TIME | |

|  | CORE BODY | UPPER BODY | LOWER BODY |
|---|---|---|---|
| EXERCISES |  |  |  |
| SETS |  |  |  |
| REPS |  |  |  |
| WEIGHTS |  |  |  |
| REST TIME |  |  |  |

|  | WARM UP | COOL DOWN |
|---|---|---|
| ACTIVITY |  |  |
| SETS |  |  |
| REPS |  |  |
| TIME |  |  |
| DIST |  |  |
| INTENSITY |  |  |

GOALS: _____

_____

_____

_____

_____

_____

_____

_____

_____

DAY: _____

NAME: _____

| | DESCRIPTION | QTY | PROTEINS | VEGGIES | FRUITS & NUTS | FATS |
|---|---|---|---|---|---|---|
| **BREAKFAST**<br><br>**TIME**<br>☐ | | | | | | |
| TOTAL | | | | | | |

| | | | | | | |
|---|---|---|---|---|---|---|
| **LUNCH**<br><br>**TIME**<br>☐ | | | | | | |
| TOTAL | | | | | | |

| | | | | | | |
|---|---|---|---|---|---|---|
| **DINNER**<br><br>**TIME**<br>☐ | | | | | | |
| TOTAL | | | | | | |

| | |
|---|---|
| **SNACKS**<br><br>**TIME**<br>☐ | |

|            | CORE BODY | UPPER BODY | LOWER BODY |
|------------|-----------|------------|------------|
| EXERCISES  |           |            |            |
| SETS       |           |            |            |
| REPS       |           |            |            |
| WEIGHTS    |           |            |            |
| REST TIME  |           |            |            |

|            | WARM UP | COOL DOWN |
|------------|---------|-----------|
| ACTIVITY   |         |           |
| SETS       |         |           |
| REPS       |         |           |
| TIME       |         |           |
| DIST       |         |           |
| INTENSITY  |         |           |

GOALS: _____

_____

_____

_____

_____

_____

_____

_____

_____

DAY: _____

NAME: _____

| | | DESCRIPTION | QTY | PROTEINS | VEGGIES | FRUITS & NUTS | FATS |
|---|---|---|---|---|---|---|---|
| **BREAKFAST** | | | | | | | |
| | | | | | | | |
| **TIME** | | | | | | | |
| | | | | | | | |
| **TOTAL** | | | | | | | |

| | | DESCRIPTION | QTY | PROTEINS | VEGGIES | FRUITS & NUTS | FATS |
|---|---|---|---|---|---|---|---|
| **LUNCH** | | | | | | | |
| | | | | | | | |
| **TIME** | | | | | | | |
| | | | | | | | |
| **TOTAL** | | | | | | | |

| | | DESCRIPTION | QTY | PROTEINS | VEGGIES | FRUITS & NUTS | FATS |
|---|---|---|---|---|---|---|---|
| **DINNER** | | | | | | | |
| | | | | | | | |
| **TIME** | | | | | | | |
| | | | | | | | |
| **TOTAL** | | | | | | | |

| | |
|---|---|
| **SNACKS** | |
| **TIME** | |

|  | CORE BODY | UPPER BODY | LOWER BODY |
|---|---|---|---|
| EXERCISES |  |  |  |
| SETS |  |  |  |
| REPS |  |  |  |
| WEIGHTS |  |  |  |
| REST TIME |  |  |  |

|  | WARM UP | COOL DOWN |
|---|---|---|
| ACTIVITY |  |  |
| SETS |  |  |
| REPS |  |  |
| TIME |  |  |
| DIST |  |  |
| INTENSITY |  |  |

GOALS: _____

_____

_____

_____

_____

_____

_____

_____

_____

DAY: _____

NAME: _____

| | | DESCRIPTION | QTY | PROTEINS | VEGGIES | FRUITS & NUTS | FATS |
|---|---|---|---|---|---|---|---|
| **BREAKFAST** | | | | | | | |
| | **TIME** | | | | | | |
| | | | | | | | |
| | **TOTAL** | | | | | | |

| | | | | | | | |
|---|---|---|---|---|---|---|---|
| **LUNCH** | | | | | | | |
| | **TIME** | | | | | | |
| | | | | | | | |
| | **TOTAL** | | | | | | |

| | | | | | | | |
|---|---|---|---|---|---|---|---|
| **DINNER** | | | | | | | |
| | **TIME** | | | | | | |
| | | | | | | | |
| | **TOTAL** | | | | | | |

| | |
|---|---|
| **SNACKS** | |
| **TIME** | |

|           | CORE BODY | UPPER BODY | LOWER BODY |
|-----------|-----------|------------|------------|
| EXERCISES |           |            |            |
| SETS      |           |            |            |
| REPS      |           |            |            |
| WEIGHTS   |           |            |            |
| REST TIME |           |            |            |

|           | WARM UP | COOL DOWN |
|-----------|---------|-----------|
| ACTIVITY  |         |           |
| SETS      |         |           |
| REPS      |         |           |
| TIME      |         |           |
| DIST      |         |           |
| INTENSITY |         |           |

GOALS: _____

_____

_____

_____

_____

_____

_____

_____

_____

DAY: _____

NAME: _____

| | DESCRIPTION | QTY | PROTEINS | VEGGIES | FRUITS & NUTS | FATS |
|---|---|---|---|---|---|---|
| **BREAKFAST**<br><br>TIME<br>⬜ | | | | | | |
| | | | | | | |
| | | | | | | |
| | | | | | | |
| TOTAL | | | | | | |

| | | | | | | |
|---|---|---|---|---|---|---|
| **LUNCH**<br><br>TIME<br>⬜ | | | | | | |
| | | | | | | |
| | | | | | | |
| | | | | | | |
| TOTAL | | | | | | |

| | | | | | | |
|---|---|---|---|---|---|---|
| **DINNER**<br><br>TIME<br>⬜ | | | | | | |
| | | | | | | |
| | | | | | | |
| | | | | | | |
| TOTAL | | | | | | |

| | |
|---|---|
| **SNACKS**<br><br>TIME<br>⬜ | |

|  | CORE BODY | UPPER BODY | LOWER BODY |
|---|---|---|---|
| EXERCISES |  |  |  |
| SETS |  |  |  |
| REPS |  |  |  |
| WEIGHTS |  |  |  |
| REST TIME |  |  |  |

|  | WARM UP | COOL DOWN |
|---|---|---|
| ACTIVITY |  |  |
| SETS |  |  |
| REPS |  |  |
| TIME |  |  |
| DIST |  |  |
| INTENSITY |  |  |

GOALS: _____

_____

_____

_____

_____

_____

_____

_____

_____

DAY: _____

NAME: _____

| | DESCRIPTION | QTY | PROTEINS | VEGGIES | FRUITS & NUTS | FATS |
|---|---|---|---|---|---|---|
| **BREAKFAST** <br><br> TIME <br> [ ] | | | | | | |
| | | | | | | |
| | | | | | | |
| | | | | | | |
| TOTAL | | | | | | |

| | | | | | | |
|---|---|---|---|---|---|---|
| **LUNCH** <br><br> TIME <br> [ ] | | | | | | |
| | | | | | | |
| | | | | | | |
| | | | | | | |
| TOTAL | | | | | | |

| | | | | | | |
|---|---|---|---|---|---|---|
| **DINNER** <br><br> TIME <br> [ ] | | | | | | |
| | | | | | | |
| | | | | | | |
| | | | | | | |
| TOTAL | | | | | | |

| | |
|---|---|
| **SNACKS** <br><br> TIME <br> [ ] | |

|  | CORE BODY | UPPER BODY | LOWER BODY |
|---|---|---|---|
| EXERCISES |  |  |  |
| SETS |  |  |  |
| REPS |  |  |  |
| WEIGHTS |  |  |  |
| REST TIME |  |  |  |

|  | WARM UP | COOL DOWN |
|---|---|---|
| ACTIVITY |  |  |
| SETS |  |  |
| REPS |  |  |
| TIME |  |  |
| DIST |  |  |
| INTENSITY |  |  |

GOALS: _____

_____

_____

_____

_____

_____

_____

_____

DAY: _____

NAME: _____

| | DESCRIPTION | QTY | PROTEINS | VEGGIES | FRUITS & NUTS | FATS |
|---|---|---|---|---|---|---|
| **BREAKFAST** <br><br> TIME <br> ☐ | | | | | | |
| | | | | | | |
| | | | | | | |
| | | | | | | |
| **TOTAL** | | | | | | |

| | | | | | | |
|---|---|---|---|---|---|---|
| **LUNCH** <br><br> TIME <br> ☐ | | | | | | |
| | | | | | | |
| | | | | | | |
| | | | | | | |
| **TOTAL** | | | | | | |

| | | | | | | |
|---|---|---|---|---|---|---|
| **DINNER** <br><br> TIME <br> ☐ | | | | | | |
| | | | | | | |
| | | | | | | |
| | | | | | | |
| **TOTAL** | | | | | | |

| | |
|---|---|
| **SNACKS** <br><br> TIME <br> ☐ | |

|  | CORE BODY | UPPER BODY | LOWER BODY |
|---|---|---|---|
| EXERCISES |  |  |  |
| SETS |  |  |  |
| REPS |  |  |  |
| WEIGHTS |  |  |  |
| REST TIME |  |  |  |

|  | WARM UP | COOL DOWN |
|---|---|---|
| ACTIVITY |  |  |
| SETS |  |  |
| REPS |  |  |
| TIME |  |  |
| DIST |  |  |
| INTENSITY |  |  |

GOALS: _____

_____

_____

_____

_____

_____

_____

_____

DAY: _____

NAME: _____

| | | DESCRIPTION | QTY | PROTEINS | VEGGIES | FRUITS & NUTS | FATS |
|---|---|---|---|---|---|---|---|
| **BREAKFAST** | | | | | | | |
| | | | | | | | |
| **TIME** | | | | | | | |
| | | | | | | | |
| **TOTAL** | | | | | | | |

| | | DESCRIPTION | QTY | PROTEINS | VEGGIES | FRUITS & NUTS | FATS |
|---|---|---|---|---|---|---|---|
| **LUNCH** | | | | | | | |
| | | | | | | | |
| **TIME** | | | | | | | |
| | | | | | | | |
| **TOTAL** | | | | | | | |

| | | DESCRIPTION | QTY | PROTEINS | VEGGIES | FRUITS & NUTS | FATS |
|---|---|---|---|---|---|---|---|
| **DINNER** | | | | | | | |
| | | | | | | | |
| **TIME** | | | | | | | |
| | | | | | | | |
| **TOTAL** | | | | | | | |

| | |
|---|---|
| **SNACKS** | |
| **TIME** | |
| | |

|  | CORE BODY | UPPER BODY | LOWER BODY |
|---|---|---|---|
| EXERCISES | | | |
| SETS | | | |
| REPS | | | |
| WEIGHTS | | | |
| REST TIME | | | |

|  | WARM UP | COOL DOWN |
|---|---|---|
| ACTIVITY | | |
| SETS | | |
| REPS | | |
| TIME | | |
| DIST | | |
| INTENSITY | | |

GOALS: _____

_____

_____

_____

_____

_____

_____

_____

DAY: _____

NAME: _____

| | | DESCRIPTION | QTY | PROTEINS | VEGGIES | FRUITS & NUTS | FATS |
|---|---|---|---|---|---|---|---|
| **BREAKFAST** | | | | | | | |
| | | | | | | | |
| **TIME** | | | | | | | |
| | | | | | | | |
| **TOTAL** | | | | | | | |

| | | DESCRIPTION | QTY | PROTEINS | VEGGIES | FRUITS & NUTS | FATS |
|---|---|---|---|---|---|---|---|
| **LUNCH** | | | | | | | |
| | | | | | | | |
| **TIME** | | | | | | | |
| | | | | | | | |
| **TOTAL** | | | | | | | |

| | | DESCRIPTION | QTY | PROTEINS | VEGGIES | FRUITS & NUTS | FATS |
|---|---|---|---|---|---|---|---|
| **DINNER** | | | | | | | |
| | | | | | | | |
| **TIME** | | | | | | | |
| | | | | | | | |
| **TOTAL** | | | | | | | |

| | |
|---|---|
| **SNACKS** | |
| **TIME** | |

|  | CORE BODY | UPPER BODY | LOWER BODY |
|---|---|---|---|
| EXERCISES |  |  |  |
| SETS |  |  |  |
| REPS |  |  |  |
| WEIGHTS |  |  |  |
| REST TIME |  |  |  |

|  | WARM UP | COOL DOWN |
|---|---|---|
| ACTIVITY |  |  |
| SETS |  |  |
| REPS |  |  |
| TIME |  |  |
| DIST |  |  |
| INTENSITY |  |  |

GOALS: _____

_____

_____

_____

_____

_____

_____

_____

_____

DAY: _____

NAME: _____

| | DESCRIPTION | QTY | PROTEINS | VEGGIES | FRUITS & NUTS | FATS |
|---|---|---|---|---|---|---|
| **BREAKFAST** | | | | | | |
| | | | | | | |
| | | | | | | |
| **TIME** | | | | | | |
| ☐ | | | | | | |
| **TOTAL** | | | | | | |

| | | | | | | |
|---|---|---|---|---|---|---|
| **LUNCH** | | | | | | |
| | | | | | | |
| | | | | | | |
| **TIME** | | | | | | |
| ☐ | | | | | | |
| **TOTAL** | | | | | | |

| | | | | | | |
|---|---|---|---|---|---|---|
| **DINNER** | | | | | | |
| | | | | | | |
| | | | | | | |
| **TIME** | | | | | | |
| ☐ | | | | | | |
| **TOTAL** | | | | | | |

| | |
|---|---|
| **SNACKS** | |
| **TIME** | |
| ☐ | |

|  | CORE BODY | UPPER BODY | LOWER BODY |
|---|---|---|---|
| EXERCISES |  |  |  |
| SETS |  |  |  |
| REPS |  |  |  |
| WEIGHTS |  |  |  |
| REST TIME |  |  |  |

|  | WARM UP | COOL DOWN |
|---|---|---|
| ACTIVITY |  |  |
| SETS |  |  |
| REPS |  |  |
| TIME |  |  |
| DIST |  |  |
| INTENSITY |  |  |

GOALS: _____

_____

_____

_____

_____

_____

_____

_____

DAY: _____

NAME: _____

| | DESCRIPTION | QTY | PROTEINS | VEGGIES | FRUITS & NUTS | FATS |
|---|---|---|---|---|---|---|
| **BREAKFAST** <br><br> **TIME** | | | | | | |
| | | | | | | |
| | | | | | | |
| | | | | | | |
| **TOTAL** | | | | | | |

| | DESCRIPTION | QTY | PROTEINS | VEGGIES | FRUITS & NUTS | FATS |
|---|---|---|---|---|---|---|
| **LUNCH** <br><br> **TIME** | | | | | | |
| | | | | | | |
| | | | | | | |
| | | | | | | |
| **TOTAL** | | | | | | |

| | DESCRIPTION | QTY | PROTEINS | VEGGIES | FRUITS & NUTS | FATS |
|---|---|---|---|---|---|---|
| **DINNER** <br><br> **TIME** | | | | | | |
| | | | | | | |
| | | | | | | |
| | | | | | | |
| **TOTAL** | | | | | | |

| | |
|---|---|
| **SNACKS** <br><br> **TIME** | |

|              | CORE BODY | UPPER BODY | LOWER BODY |
|--------------|-----------|------------|------------|
| EXERCISES    |           |            |            |
| SETS         |           |            |            |
| REPS         |           |            |            |
| WEIGHTS      |           |            |            |
| REST TIME    |           |            |            |

|            | WARM UP | COOL DOWN |
|------------|---------|-----------|
| ACTIVITY   |         |           |
| SETS       |         |           |
| REPS       |         |           |
| TIME       |         |           |
| DIST       |         |           |
| INTENSITY  |         |           |

GOALS: _____

_____

_____

_____

_____

_____

_____

_____

_____

DAY: _____

NAME: _____

| | | DESCRIPTION | QTY | PROTEINS | VEGGIES | FRUITS & NUTS | FATS |
|---|---|---|---|---|---|---|---|
| **BREAKFAST** | | | | | | | |
| | | | | | | | |
| **TIME** | | | | | | | |
| | | | | | | | |
| **TOTAL** | | | | | | | |

| | | DESCRIPTION | QTY | PROTEINS | VEGGIES | FRUITS & NUTS | FATS |
|---|---|---|---|---|---|---|---|
| **LUNCH** | | | | | | | |
| | | | | | | | |
| **TIME** | | | | | | | |
| | | | | | | | |
| **TOTAL** | | | | | | | |

| | | DESCRIPTION | QTY | PROTEINS | VEGGIES | FRUITS & NUTS | FATS |
|---|---|---|---|---|---|---|---|
| **DINNER** | | | | | | | |
| | | | | | | | |
| **TIME** | | | | | | | |
| | | | | | | | |
| **TOTAL** | | | | | | | |

| | |
|---|---|
| **SNACKS** | |
| **TIME** | |
| | |

|  | CORE BODY | UPPER BODY | LOWER BODY |
|---|---|---|---|
| EXERCISES | | | |
| SETS | | | |
| REPS | | | |
| WEIGHTS | | | |
| REST TIME | | | |

|  | WARM UP | COOL DOWN |
|---|---|---|
| ACTIVITY | | |
| SETS | | |
| REPS | | |
| TIME | | |
| DIST | | |
| INTENSITY | | |

GOALS: _____

_____

_____

_____

_____

_____

_____

_____

_____

DAY: _____

NAME: _____

| | | DESCRIPTION | QTY | PROTEINS | VEGGIES | FRUITS & NUTS | FATS |
|---|---|---|---|---|---|---|---|
| BREAKFAST | | | | | | | |
| TIME | | | | | | | |
| | | | | | | | |
| TOTAL | | | | | | | |

| | | | | | | | |
|---|---|---|---|---|---|---|---|
| LUNCH | | | | | | | |
| TIME | | | | | | | |
| | | | | | | | |
| TOTAL | | | | | | | |

| | | | | | | | |
|---|---|---|---|---|---|---|---|
| DINNER | | | | | | | |
| TIME | | | | | | | |
| | | | | | | | |
| TOTAL | | | | | | | |

| | |
|---|---|
| SNACKS | |
| TIME | |

|  | CORE BODY | UPPER BODY | LOWER BODY |
|---|---|---|---|
| EXERCISES | | | |
| SETS | | | |
| REPS | | | |
| WEIGHTS | | | |
| REST TIME | | | |

|  | WARM UP | COOL DOWN |
|---|---|---|
| ACTIVITY | | |
| SETS | | |
| REPS | | |
| TIME | | |
| DIST | | |
| INTENSITY | | |

GOALS: _____

_____

_____

_____

_____

_____

_____

_____

_____

DAY: _____

NAME: _____

| | DESCRIPTION | QTY | PROTEINS | VEGGIES | FRUITS & NUTS | FATS |
|---|---|---|---|---|---|---|
| **BREAKFAST** | | | | | | |
| | | | | | | |
| TIME | | | | | | |
| | | | | | | |
| TOTAL | | | | | | |

| | | | | | | |
|---|---|---|---|---|---|---|
| **LUNCH** | | | | | | |
| | | | | | | |
| TIME | | | | | | |
| | | | | | | |
| TOTAL | | | | | | |

| | | | | | | |
|---|---|---|---|---|---|---|
| **DINNER** | | | | | | |
| | | | | | | |
| TIME | | | | | | |
| | | | | | | |
| TOTAL | | | | | | |

| | |
|---|---|
| **SNACKS** | |
| TIME | |

|            | CORE BODY | UPPER BODY | LOWER BODY |
|------------|-----------|------------|------------|
| EXERCISES  |           |            |            |
| SETS       |           |            |            |
| REPS       |           |            |            |
| WEIGHTS    |           |            |            |
| REST TIME  |           |            |            |

|            | WARM UP | COOL DOWN |
|------------|---------|-----------|
| ACTIVITY   |         |           |
| SETS       |         |           |
| REPS       |         |           |
| TIME       |         |           |
| DIST       |         |           |
| INTENSITY  |         |           |

GOALS: _____

_____

_____

_____

_____

_____

_____

_____

DAY: _____

NAME: _____

| | DESCRIPTION | QTY | PROTEINS | VEGGIES | FRUITS & NUTS | FATS |
|---|---|---|---|---|---|---|
| **BREAKFAST** <br><br> TIME <br> ☐ | | | | | | |
| TOTAL | | | | | | |

| | | | | | | |
|---|---|---|---|---|---|---|
| **LUNCH** <br><br> TIME <br> ☐ | | | | | | |
| TOTAL | | | | | | |

| | | | | | | |
|---|---|---|---|---|---|---|
| **DINNER** <br><br> TIME <br> ☐ | | | | | | |
| TOTAL | | | | | | |

| | |
|---|---|
| **SNACKS** <br><br> TIME <br> ☐ | |

|  | CORE BODY | UPPER BODY | LOWER BODY |
|---|---|---|---|
| EXERCISES |  |  |  |
| SETS |  |  |  |
| REPS |  |  |  |
| WEIGHTS |  |  |  |
| REST TIME |  |  |  |

|  | WARM UP | COOL DOWN |
|---|---|---|
| ACTIVITY |  |  |
| SETS |  |  |
| REPS |  |  |
| TIME |  |  |
| DIST |  |  |
| INTENSITY |  |  |

GOALS: _____

_____

_____

_____

_____

_____

_____

_____

_____

DAY: _____

NAME: _____

| | DESCRIPTION | QTY | PROTEINS | VEGGIES | FRUITS & NUTS | FATS |
|---|---|---|---|---|---|---|
| **BREAKFAST** <br><br> TIME <br> [ ] | | | | | | |
| TOTAL | | | | | | |

| | | | | | | |
|---|---|---|---|---|---|---|
| **LUNCH** <br><br> TIME <br> [ ] | | | | | | |
| TOTAL | | | | | | |

| | | | | | | |
|---|---|---|---|---|---|---|
| **DINNER** <br><br> TIME <br> [ ] | | | | | | |
| TOTAL | | | | | | |

| | |
|---|---|
| **SNACKS** <br><br> TIME <br> [ ] | |

|              | CORE BODY | UPPER BODY | LOWER BODY |
|--------------|-----------|------------|------------|
| EXERCISES    |           |            |            |
| SETS         |           |            |            |
| REPS         |           |            |            |
| WEIGHTS      |           |            |            |
| REST TIME    |           |            |            |

|           | WARM UP | COOL DOWN |
|-----------|---------|-----------|
| ACTIVITY  |         |           |
| SETS      |         |           |
| REPS      |         |           |
| TIME      |         |           |
| DIST      |         |           |
| INTENSITY |         |           |

GOALS: _____

_____

_____

_____

_____

_____

_____

_____

_____

DAY: _____

NAME: _____

| | DESCRIPTION | QTY | PROTEINS | VEGGIES | FRUITS & NUTS | FATS |
|---|---|---|---|---|---|---|
| **BREAKFAST**<br><br>TIME<br>[ ] | | | | | | |
| | | | | | | |
| | | | | | | |
| | | | | | | |
| TOTAL | | | | | | |

| | | | | | | |
|---|---|---|---|---|---|---|
| **LUNCH**<br><br>TIME<br>[ ] | | | | | | |
| | | | | | | |
| | | | | | | |
| | | | | | | |
| TOTAL | | | | | | |

| | | | | | | |
|---|---|---|---|---|---|---|
| **DINNER**<br><br>TIME<br>[ ] | | | | | | |
| | | | | | | |
| | | | | | | |
| | | | | | | |
| TOTAL | | | | | | |

| | |
|---|---|
| **SNACKS**<br><br>TIME<br>[ ] | |

|  | CORE BODY | UPPER BODY | LOWER BODY |
|---|---|---|---|
| EXERCISES |  |  |  |
| SETS |  |  |  |
| REPS |  |  |  |
| WEIGHTS |  |  |  |
| REST TIME |  |  |  |

|  | WARM UP | COOL DOWN |
|---|---|---|
| ACTIVITY |  |  |
| SETS |  |  |
| REPS |  |  |
| TIME |  |  |
| DIST |  |  |
| INTENSITY |  |  |

GOALS: _____

_____

_____

_____

_____

_____

_____

_____

_____

DAY: _____

NAME: _____

| | DESCRIPTION | QTY | PROTEINS | VEGGIES | FRUITS & NUTS | FATS |
|---|---|---|---|---|---|---|
| **BREAKFAST**<br><br>TIME<br>[　] | | | | | | |
| | | | | | | |
| | | | | | | |
| | | | | | | |
| TOTAL | | | | | | |

| | | | | | | |
|---|---|---|---|---|---|---|
| **LUNCH**<br><br>TIME<br>[　] | | | | | | |
| | | | | | | |
| | | | | | | |
| TOTAL | | | | | | |

| | | | | | | |
|---|---|---|---|---|---|---|
| **DINNER**<br><br>TIME<br>[　] | | | | | | |
| | | | | | | |
| | | | | | | |
| TOTAL | | | | | | |

| | |
|---|---|
| **SNACKS**<br><br>TIME<br>[　] | |

|  | CORE BODY | UPPER BODY | LOWER BODY |
|---|---|---|---|
| EXERCISES | | | |
| SETS | | | |
| REPS | | | |
| WEIGHTS | | | |
| REST TIME | | | |

|  | WARM UP | COOL DOWN |
|---|---|---|
| ACTIVITY | | |
| SETS | | |
| REPS | | |
| TIME | | |
| DIST | | |
| INTENSITY | | |

GOALS: _____

_____

_____

_____

_____

_____

_____

_____

_____

DAY: _____

NAME: _____

| | DESCRIPTION | QTY | PROTEINS | VEGGIES | FRUITS & NUTS | FATS |
|---|---|---|---|---|---|---|
| **BREAKFAST** | | | | | | |
| | | | | | | |
| **TIME** | | | | | | |
| | | | | | | |
| **TOTAL** | | | | | | |

| | | | | | | |
|---|---|---|---|---|---|---|
| **LUNCH** | | | | | | |
| | | | | | | |
| **TIME** | | | | | | |
| | | | | | | |
| **TOTAL** | | | | | | |

| | | | | | | |
|---|---|---|---|---|---|---|
| **DINNER** | | | | | | |
| | | | | | | |
| **TIME** | | | | | | |
| | | | | | | |
| **TOTAL** | | | | | | |

| | |
|---|---|
| **SNACKS** | |
| **TIME** | |

|  | CORE BODY | UPPER BODY | LOWER BODY |
|---|---|---|---|
| EXERCISES |  |  |  |
| SETS |  |  |  |
| REPS |  |  |  |
| WEIGHTS |  |  |  |
| REST TIME |  |  |  |

|  | WARM UP | COOL DOWN |
|---|---|---|
| ACTIVITY |  |  |
| SETS |  |  |
| REPS |  |  |
| TIME |  |  |
| DIST |  |  |
| INTENSITY |  |  |

GOALS: _____

_____

_____

_____

_____

_____

_____

_____

_____

DAY: _____

NAME: _____

| | DESCRIPTION | QTY | PROTEINS | VEGGIES | FRUITS & NUTS | FATS |
|---|---|---|---|---|---|---|
| **BREAKFAST** | | | | | | |
| TIME | | | | | | |
| TOTAL | | | | | | |

| | | | | | | |
|---|---|---|---|---|---|---|
| **LUNCH** | | | | | | |
| TIME | | | | | | |
| TOTAL | | | | | | |

| | | | | | | |
|---|---|---|---|---|---|---|
| **DINNER** | | | | | | |
| TIME | | | | | | |
| TOTAL | | | | | | |

| | |
|---|---|
| **SNACKS** | |
| TIME | |

|  | CORE BODY | UPPER BODY | LOWER BODY |
|---|---|---|---|
| EXERCISES | | | |
| SETS | | | |
| REPS | | | |
| WEIGHTS | | | |
| REST TIME | | | |

|  | WARM UP | COOL DOWN |
|---|---|---|
| ACTIVITY | | |
| SETS | | |
| REPS | | |
| TIME | | |
| DIST | | |
| INTENSITY | | |

GOALS: _____

_____

_____

_____

_____

_____

_____

_____

_____

DAY: _____

NAME: _____

| | | DESCRIPTION | QTY | PROTEINS | VEGGIES | FRUITS & NUTS | FATS |
|---|---|---|---|---|---|---|---|
| BREAKFAST | | | | | | | |
| TIME | | | | | | | |
| | | | | | | | |
| TOTAL | | | | | | | |

| | | | | | | | |
|---|---|---|---|---|---|---|---|
| LUNCH | | | | | | | |
| TIME | | | | | | | |
| | | | | | | | |
| TOTAL | | | | | | | |

| | | | | | | | |
|---|---|---|---|---|---|---|---|
| DINNER | | | | | | | |
| TIME | | | | | | | |
| | | | | | | | |
| TOTAL | | | | | | | |

| | |
|---|---|
| SNACKS | |
| TIME | |

|  | CORE BODY | UPPER BODY | LOWER BODY |
|---|---|---|---|
| EXERCISES |  |  |  |
| SETS |  |  |  |
| REPS |  |  |  |
| WEIGHTS |  |  |  |
| REST TIME |  |  |  |

|  | WARM UP | COOL DOWN |
|---|---|---|
| ACTIVITY |  |  |
| SETS |  |  |
| REPS |  |  |
| TIME |  |  |
| DIST |  |  |
| INTENSITY |  |  |

GOALS: _____

_____

_____

_____

_____

_____

_____

_____

_____

DAY: _____

NAME: _____

| | DESCRIPTION | QTY | PROTEINS | VEGGIES | FRUITS & NUTS | FATS |
|---|---|---|---|---|---|---|
| **BREAKFAST**<br><br>TIME | | | | | | |
| | | | | | | |
| | | | | | | |
| | | | | | | |
| TOTAL | | | | | | |

| | | | | | | |
|---|---|---|---|---|---|---|
| **LUNCH**<br><br>TIME | | | | | | |
| | | | | | | |
| | | | | | | |
| | | | | | | |
| TOTAL | | | | | | |

| | | | | | | |
|---|---|---|---|---|---|---|
| **DINNER**<br><br>TIME | | | | | | |
| | | | | | | |
| | | | | | | |
| | | | | | | |
| TOTAL | | | | | | |

| | |
|---|---|
| **SNACKS**<br><br>TIME | |

|            | CORE BODY | UPPER BODY | LOWER BODY |
|------------|-----------|------------|------------|
| EXERCISES  |           |            |            |
| SETS       |           |            |            |
| REPS       |           |            |            |
| WEIGHTS    |           |            |            |
| REST TIME  |           |            |            |

|            | WARM UP | COOL DOWN |
|------------|---------|-----------|
| ACTIVITY   |         |           |
| SETS       |         |           |
| REPS       |         |           |
| TIME       |         |           |
| DIST       |         |           |
| INTENSITY  |         |           |

GOALS: _____

_____

_____

_____

_____

_____

_____

_____

DAY: _____

NAME: _____

| | | DESCRIPTION | QTY | PROTEINS | VEGGIES | FRUITS & NUTS | FATS |
|---|---|---|---|---|---|---|---|
| **BREAKFAST** | | | | | | | |
| | | | | | | | |
| **TIME** | | | | | | | |
| | | | | | | | |
| **TOTAL** | | | | | | | |

| | | DESCRIPTION | QTY | PROTEINS | VEGGIES | FRUITS & NUTS | FATS |
|---|---|---|---|---|---|---|---|
| **LUNCH** | | | | | | | |
| | | | | | | | |
| **TIME** | | | | | | | |
| | | | | | | | |
| **TOTAL** | | | | | | | |

| | | DESCRIPTION | QTY | PROTEINS | VEGGIES | FRUITS & NUTS | FATS |
|---|---|---|---|---|---|---|---|
| **DINNER** | | | | | | | |
| | | | | | | | |
| **TIME** | | | | | | | |
| | | | | | | | |
| **TOTAL** | | | | | | | |

| | |
|---|---|
| **SNACKS** | |
| **TIME** | |

|  | CORE BODY | UPPER BODY | LOWER BODY |
|---|---|---|---|
| EXERCISES |  |  |  |
| SETS |  |  |  |
| REPS |  |  |  |
| WEIGHTS |  |  |  |
| REST TIME |  |  |  |

|  | WARM UP | COOL DOWN |
|---|---|---|
| ACTIVITY |  |  |
| SETS |  |  |
| REPS |  |  |
| TIME |  |  |
| DIST |  |  |
| INTENSITY |  |  |

GOALS: _____

_____

_____

_____

_____

_____

_____

_____

_____

DAY: _____

NAME: _____

| | DESCRIPTION | QTY | PROTEINS | VEGGIES | FRUITS & NUTS | FATS |
|---|---|---|---|---|---|---|
| **BREAKFAST**<br><br>TIME | | | | | | |
| | | | | | | |
| | | | | | | |
| | | | | | | |
| **TOTAL** | | | | | | |

| | | | | | | |
|---|---|---|---|---|---|---|
| **LUNCH**<br><br>TIME | | | | | | |
| | | | | | | |
| | | | | | | |
| | | | | | | |
| **TOTAL** | | | | | | |

| | | | | | | |
|---|---|---|---|---|---|---|
| **DINNER**<br><br>TIME | | | | | | |
| | | | | | | |
| | | | | | | |
| | | | | | | |
| **TOTAL** | | | | | | |

| | |
|---|---|
| **SNACKS**<br><br>TIME | |

|  | CORE BODY | UPPER BODY | LOWER BODY |
|---|---|---|---|
| EXERCISES |  |  |  |
| SETS |  |  |  |
| REPS |  |  |  |
| WEIGHTS |  |  |  |
| REST TIME |  |  |  |

|  | WARM UP | COOL DOWN |
|---|---|---|
| ACTIVITY |  |  |
| SETS |  |  |
| REPS |  |  |
| TIME |  |  |
| DIST |  |  |
| INTENSITY |  |  |

GOALS: _____

_____

_____

_____

_____

_____

_____

_____

DAY: _____

NAME: _____

| | DESCRIPTION | QTY | PROTEINS | VEGGIES | FRUITS & NUTS | FATS |
|---|---|---|---|---|---|---|
| **BREAKFAST** | | | | | | |
| | | | | | | |
| | | | | | | |
| **TIME** | | | | | | |
| **TOTAL** | | | | | | |

| | | | | | | |
|---|---|---|---|---|---|---|
| **LUNCH** | | | | | | |
| | | | | | | |
| | | | | | | |
| **TIME** | | | | | | |
| **TOTAL** | | | | | | |

| | | | | | | |
|---|---|---|---|---|---|---|
| **DINNER** | | | | | | |
| | | | | | | |
| | | | | | | |
| **TIME** | | | | | | |
| **TOTAL** | | | | | | |

| | |
|---|---|
| **SNACKS** | |
| | |
| **TIME** | |

|  | CORE BODY | UPPER BODY | LOWER BODY |
|---|---|---|---|
| EXERCISES |  |  |  |
| SETS |  |  |  |
| REPS |  |  |  |
| WEIGHTS |  |  |  |
| REST TIME |  |  |  |

|  | WARM UP | COOL DOWN |
|---|---|---|
| ACTIVITY |  |  |
| SETS |  |  |
| REPS |  |  |
| TIME |  |  |
| DIST |  |  |
| INTENSITY |  |  |

GOALS: _____

_____

_____

_____

_____

_____

_____

_____

DAY: _____

NAME: _____

| | DESCRIPTION | QTY | PROTEINS | VEGGIES | FRUITS & NUTS | FATS |
|---|---|---|---|---|---|---|
| **BREAKFAST** | | | | | | |
| | | | | | | |
| **TIME** | | | | | | |
| | | | | | | |
| **TOTAL** | | | | | | |

| | DESCRIPTION | QTY | PROTEINS | VEGGIES | FRUITS & NUTS | FATS |
|---|---|---|---|---|---|---|
| **LUNCH** | | | | | | |
| | | | | | | |
| **TIME** | | | | | | |
| | | | | | | |
| **TOTAL** | | | | | | |

| | DESCRIPTION | QTY | PROTEINS | VEGGIES | FRUITS & NUTS | FATS |
|---|---|---|---|---|---|---|
| **DINNER** | | | | | | |
| | | | | | | |
| **TIME** | | | | | | |
| | | | | | | |
| **TOTAL** | | | | | | |

| | |
|---|---|
| **SNACKS** | |
| | |
| **TIME** | |
| | |

|  | CORE BODY | UPPER BODY | LOWER BODY |
|---|---|---|---|
| EXERCISES |  |  |  |
| SETS |  |  |  |
| REPS |  |  |  |
| WEIGHTS |  |  |  |
| REST TIME |  |  |  |

|  | WARM UP | COOL DOWN |
|---|---|---|
| ACTIVITY |  |  |
| SETS |  |  |
| REPS |  |  |
| TIME |  |  |
| DIST |  |  |
| INTENSITY |  |  |

GOALS: _____

_____

_____

_____

_____

_____

_____

_____

_____

DAY: _____

NAME: _____

| | | DESCRIPTION | QTY | PROTEINS | VEGGIES | FRUITS & NUTS | FATS |
|---|---|---|---|---|---|---|---|
| **BREAKFAST** | | | | | | | |
| | | | | | | | |
| TIME | | | | | | | |
| | | | | | | | |
| TOTAL | | | | | | | |

| | | | | | | | |
|---|---|---|---|---|---|---|---|
| LUNCH | | | | | | | |
| | | | | | | | |
| TIME | | | | | | | |
| | | | | | | | |
| TOTAL | | | | | | | |

| | | | | | | | |
|---|---|---|---|---|---|---|---|
| **DINNER** | | | | | | | |
| | | | | | | | |
| TIME | | | | | | | |
| | | | | | | | |
| TOTAL | | | | | | | |

| | |
|---|---|
| **SNACKS** | |
| TIME | |

|  | CORE BODY | UPPER BODY | LOWER BODY |
|---|---|---|---|
| EXERCISES |  |  |  |
| SETS |  |  |  |
| REPS |  |  |  |
| WEIGHTS |  |  |  |
| REST TIME |  |  |  |

|  | WARM UP | COOL DOWN |
|---|---|---|
| ACTIVITY |  |  |
| SETS |  |  |
| REPS |  |  |
| TIME |  |  |
| DIST |  |  |
| INTENSITY |  |  |

GOALS: _____

_____

_____

_____

_____

_____

_____

_____

_____

_____

DAY: _____

NAME: _____

| | DESCRIPTION | QTY | PROTEINS | VEGGIES | FRUITS & NUTS | FATS |
|---|---|---|---|---|---|---|
| **BREAKFAST** | | | | | | |
| | | | | | | |
| **TIME** | | | | | | |
| | | | | | | |
| **TOTAL** | | | | | | |

| | | | | | | |
|---|---|---|---|---|---|---|
| **LUNCH** | | | | | | |
| | | | | | | |
| **TIME** | | | | | | |
| | | | | | | |
| **TOTAL** | | | | | | |

| | | | | | | |
|---|---|---|---|---|---|---|
| **DINNER** | | | | | | |
| | | | | | | |
| **TIME** | | | | | | |
| | | | | | | |
| **TOTAL** | | | | | | |

| | |
|---|---|
| **SNACKS** | |
| **TIME** | |

|  | CORE BODY | UPPER BODY | LOWER BODY |
| --- | --- | --- | --- |
| EXERCISES |  |  |  |
| SETS |  |  |  |
| REPS |  |  |  |
| WEIGHTS |  |  |  |
| REST TIME |  |  |  |

|  | WARM UP | COOL DOWN |
| --- | --- | --- |
| ACTIVITY |  |  |
| SETS |  |  |
| REPS |  |  |
| TIME |  |  |
| DIST |  |  |
| INTENSITY |  |  |

GOALS: _____

_____

_____

_____

_____

_____

_____

_____

_____

DAY: _____

NAME: _____

| | | DESCRIPTION | QTY | PROTEINS | VEGGIES | FRUITS & NUTS | FATS |
|---|---|---|---|---|---|---|---|
| **BREAKFAST** | | | | | | | |
| **TIME** | | | | | | | |
| | | | | | | | |
| **TOTAL** | | | | | | | |

| | | | | | | | |
|---|---|---|---|---|---|---|---|
| **LUNCH** | | | | | | | |
| **TIME** | | | | | | | |
| | | | | | | | |
| **TOTAL** | | | | | | | |

| | | | | | | | |
|---|---|---|---|---|---|---|---|
| **DINNER** | | | | | | | |
| **TIME** | | | | | | | |
| | | | | | | | |
| **TOTAL** | | | | | | | |

| | |
|---|---|
| **SNACKS** | |
| **TIME** | |

|  | CORE BODY | UPPER BODY | LOWER BODY |
|---|---|---|---|
| EXERCISES |  |  |  |
| SETS |  |  |  |
| REPS |  |  |  |
| WEIGHTS |  |  |  |
| REST TIME |  |  |  |

|  | WARM UP | COOL DOWN |
|---|---|---|
| ACTIVITY |  |  |
| SETS |  |  |
| REPS |  |  |
| TIME |  |  |
| DIST |  |  |
| INTENSITY |  |  |

GOALS: _____

_____

_____

_____

_____

_____

_____

_____

DAY: _____

NAME: _____

| | | DESCRIPTION | QTY | PROTEINS | VEGGIES | FRUITS & NUTS | FATS |
|---|---|---|---|---|---|---|---|
| **BREAKFAST** | | | | | | | |
| | | | | | | | |
| **TIME** | | | | | | | |
| | | | | | | | |
| **TOTAL** | | | | | | | |

| | | DESCRIPTION | QTY | PROTEINS | VEGGIES | FRUITS & NUTS | FATS |
|---|---|---|---|---|---|---|---|
| **LUNCH** | | | | | | | |
| | | | | | | | |
| **TIME** | | | | | | | |
| | | | | | | | |
| **TOTAL** | | | | | | | |

| | | DESCRIPTION | QTY | PROTEINS | VEGGIES | FRUITS & NUTS | FATS |
|---|---|---|---|---|---|---|---|
| **DINNER** | | | | | | | |
| | | | | | | | |
| **TIME** | | | | | | | |
| | | | | | | | |
| **TOTAL** | | | | | | | |

| | |
|---|---|
| **SNACKS** | |
| **TIME** | |

|  | CORE BODY | UPPER BODY | LOWER BODY |
|---|---|---|---|
| EXERCISES |  |  |  |
| SETS |  |  |  |
| REPS |  |  |  |
| WEIGHTS |  |  |  |
| REST TIME |  |  |  |

|  | WARM UP | COOL DOWN |
|---|---|---|
| ACTIVITY |  |  |
| SETS |  |  |
| REPS |  |  |
| TIME |  |  |
| DIST |  |  |
| INTENSITY |  |  |

GOALS: _____

_____

_____

_____

_____

_____

_____

_____

_____

DAY: _____

NAME: _____

| | | DESCRIPTION | QTY | PROTEINS | VEGGIES | FRUITS & NUTS | FATS |
|---|---|---|---|---|---|---|---|
| **BREAKFAST** | | | | | | | |
| | **TIME** | | | | | | |
| | | | | | | | |
| | **TOTAL** | | | | | | |

| | | | | | | | |
|---|---|---|---|---|---|---|---|
| **LUNCH** | | | | | | | |
| | **TIME** | | | | | | |
| | | | | | | | |
| | **TOTAL** | | | | | | |

| | | | | | | | |
|---|---|---|---|---|---|---|---|
| **DINNER** | | | | | | | |
| | **TIME** | | | | | | |
| | | | | | | | |
| | **TOTAL** | | | | | | |

| | |
|---|---|
| **SNACKS** | |
| **TIME** | |

|  | CORE BODY | UPPER BODY | LOWER BODY |
|---|---|---|---|
| EXERCISES |  |  |  |
| SETS |  |  |  |
| REPS |  |  |  |
| WEIGHTS |  |  |  |
| REST TIME |  |  |  |

|  | WARM UP | COOL DOWN |
|---|---|---|
| ACTIVITY |  |  |
| SETS |  |  |
| REPS |  |  |
| TIME |  |  |
| DIST |  |  |
| INTENSITY |  |  |

GOALS: _____

_____

_____

_____

_____

_____

_____

_____

_____

DAY: _____

NAME: _____

| | | DESCRIPTION | QTY | PROTEINS | VEGGIES | FRUITS & NUTS | FATS |
|---|---|---|---|---|---|---|---|
| **BREAKFAST** | | | | | | | |
| | | | | | | | |
| **TIME** | | | | | | | |
| | | | | | | | |
| **TOTAL** | | | | | | | |

| | | | | | | | |
|---|---|---|---|---|---|---|---|
| **LUNCH** | | | | | | | |
| | | | | | | | |
| **TIME** | | | | | | | |
| | | | | | | | |
| **TOTAL** | | | | | | | |

| | | | | | | | |
|---|---|---|---|---|---|---|---|
| **DINNER** | | | | | | | |
| | | | | | | | |
| **TIME** | | | | | | | |
| | | | | | | | |
| **TOTAL** | | | | | | | |

| | |
|---|---|
| **SNACKS** | |
| **TIME** | |

|  | CORE BODY | UPPER BODY | LOWER BODY |
|---|---|---|---|
| EXERCISES |  |  |  |
| SETS |  |  |  |
| REPS |  |  |  |
| WEIGHTS |  |  |  |
| REST TIME |  |  |  |

|  | WARM UP | COOL DOWN |
|---|---|---|
| ACTIVITY |  |  |
| SETS |  |  |
| REPS |  |  |
| TIME |  |  |
| DIST |  |  |
| INTENSITY |  |  |

GOALS: _____

_____

_____

_____

_____

_____

_____

_____

DAY: _____

NAME: _____

| | DESCRIPTION | QTY | PROTEINS | VEGGIES | FRUITS & NUTS | FATS |
|---|---|---|---|---|---|---|
| **BREAKFAST** <br><br> TIME <br> [ ] | | | | | | |
| TOTAL | | | | | | |

| | | | | | | |
|---|---|---|---|---|---|---|
| **LUNCH** <br><br> TIME <br> [ ] | | | | | | |
| TOTAL | | | | | | |

| | | | | | | |
|---|---|---|---|---|---|---|
| **DINNER** <br><br> TIME <br> [ ] | | | | | | |
| TOTAL | | | | | | |

| | |
|---|---|
| **SNACKS** <br><br> TIME <br> [ ] | |

|              | CORE BODY | UPPER BODY | LOWER BODY |
|--------------|-----------|------------|------------|
| EXERCISES    |           |            |            |
| SETS         |           |            |            |
| REPS         |           |            |            |
| WEIGHTS      |           |            |            |
| REST TIME    |           |            |            |

|              | WARM UP | COOL DOWN |
|--------------|---------|-----------|
| ACTIVITY     |         |           |
| SETS         |         |           |
| REPS         |         |           |
| TIME         |         |           |
| DIST         |         |           |
| INTENSITY    |         |           |

GOALS: _____

_____

_____

_____

_____

_____

_____

_____

_____

DAY: _____

NAME: _____

| | | DESCRIPTION | QTY | PROTEINS | VEGGIES | FRUITS & NUTS | FATS |
|---|---|---|---|---|---|---|---|
| BREAKFAST | | | | | | | |
| | | | | | | | |
| TIME | | | | | | | |
| | | | | | | | |
| TOTAL | | | | | | | |

| | | | | | | | |
|---|---|---|---|---|---|---|---|
| LUNCH | | | | | | | |
| | | | | | | | |
| TIME | | | | | | | |
| | | | | | | | |
| TOTAL | | | | | | | |

| | | | | | | | |
|---|---|---|---|---|---|---|---|
| DINNER | | | | | | | |
| | | | | | | | |
| TIME | | | | | | | |
| | | | | | | | |
| TOTAL | | | | | | | |

| | |
|---|---|
| SNACKS | |
| TIME | |

|  | CORE BODY | UPPER BODY | LOWER BODY |
|---|---|---|---|
| EXERCISES | | | |
| SETS | | | |
| REPS | | | |
| WEIGHTS | | | |
| REST TIME | | | |

|  | WARM UP | COOL DOWN |
|---|---|---|
| ACTIVITY | | |
| SETS | | |
| REPS | | |
| TIME | | |
| DIST | | |
| INTENSITY | | |

GOALS: _____

_____

_____

_____

_____

_____

_____

_____

DAY: _____

NAME: _____

| | | DESCRIPTION | QTY | PROTEINS | VEGGIES | FRUITS & NUTS | FATS |
|---|---|---|---|---|---|---|---|
| **BREAKFAST** | | | | | | | |
| | | | | | | | |
| **TIME** | | | | | | | |
| | | | | | | | |
| **TOTAL** | | | | | | | |

| | | | | | | | |
|---|---|---|---|---|---|---|---|
| **LUNCH** | | | | | | | |
| | | | | | | | |
| **TIME** | | | | | | | |
| | | | | | | | |
| **TOTAL** | | | | | | | |

| | | | | | | | |
|---|---|---|---|---|---|---|---|
| **DINNER** | | | | | | | |
| | | | | | | | |
| **TIME** | | | | | | | |
| | | | | | | | |
| **TOTAL** | | | | | | | |

| | |
|---|---|
| **SNACKS** | |
| **TIME** | |

|  | CORE BODY | UPPER BODY | LOWER BODY |
|---|---|---|---|
| EXERCISES |  |  |  |
| SETS |  |  |  |
| REPS |  |  |  |
| WEIGHTS |  |  |  |
| REST TIME |  |  |  |

|  | WARM UP | COOL DOWN |
|---|---|---|
| ACTIVITY |  |  |
| SETS |  |  |
| REPS |  |  |
| TIME |  |  |
| DIST |  |  |
| INTENSITY |  |  |

GOALS: _____

_____

_____

_____

_____

_____

_____

_____

DAY: _____

NAME: _____

| | DESCRIPTION | QTY | PROTEINS | VEGGIES | FRUITS & NUTS | FATS |
|---|---|---|---|---|---|---|
| **BREAKFAST** | | | | | | |
| | | | | | | |
| **TIME** | | | | | | |
| ☐ | | | | | | |
| **TOTAL** | | | | | | |

| | | | | | | |
|---|---|---|---|---|---|---|
| **LUNCH** | | | | | | |
| | | | | | | |
| **TIME** | | | | | | |
| ☐ | | | | | | |
| **TOTAL** | | | | | | |

| | | | | | | |
|---|---|---|---|---|---|---|
| **DINNER** | | | | | | |
| | | | | | | |
| **TIME** | | | | | | |
| ☐ | | | | | | |
| **TOTAL** | | | | | | |

| | |
|---|---|
| **SNACKS** | |
| **TIME** | |
| ☐ | |

|            | CORE BODY | UPPER BODY | LOWER BODY |
|------------|-----------|------------|------------|
| EXERCISES  |           |            |            |
| SETS       |           |            |            |
| REPS       |           |            |            |
| WEIGHTS    |           |            |            |
| REST TIME  |           |            |            |

|            | WARM UP | COOL DOWN |
|------------|---------|-----------|
| ACTIVITY   |         |           |
| SETS       |         |           |
| REPS       |         |           |
| TIME       |         |           |
| DIST       |         |           |
| INTENSITY  |         |           |

GOALS: _____

_____

_____

_____

_____

_____

_____

_____

DAY: _____

NAME: _____

| | | DESCRIPTION | QTY | PROTEINS | VEGGIES | FRUITS & NUTS | FATS |
|---|---|---|---|---|---|---|---|
| **BREAKFAST** | | | | | | | |
| **TIME** | | | | | | | |
| **TOTAL** | | | | | | | |

| | | | | | | | |
|---|---|---|---|---|---|---|---|
| **LUNCH** | | | | | | | |
| **TIME** | | | | | | | |
| **TOTAL** | | | | | | | |

| | | | | | | | |
|---|---|---|---|---|---|---|---|
| **DINNER** | | | | | | | |
| **TIME** | | | | | | | |
| **TOTAL** | | | | | | | |

| | |
|---|---|
| **SNACKS** | |
| **TIME** | |

|  | CORE BODY | UPPER BODY | LOWER BODY |
|---|---|---|---|
| EXERCISES | | | |
| SETS | | | |
| REPS | | | |
| WEIGHTS | | | |
| REST TIME | | | |

|  | WARM UP | COOL DOWN |
|---|---|---|
| ACTIVITY | | |
| SETS | | |
| REPS | | |
| TIME | | |
| DIST | | |
| INTENSITY | | |

GOALS: _____

_____

_____

_____

_____

_____

_____

_____

_____

DAY: _____

NAME: _____

| | DESCRIPTION | QTY | PROTEINS | VEGGIES | FRUITS & NUTS | FATS |
|---|---|---|---|---|---|---|
| **BREAKFAST** <br><br> **TIME** <br> [ ] | | | | | | |
| TOTAL | | | | | | |

| | | | | | | |
|---|---|---|---|---|---|---|
| **LUNCH** <br><br> **TIME** <br> [ ] | | | | | | |
| TOTAL | | | | | | |

| | | | | | | |
|---|---|---|---|---|---|---|
| **DINNER** <br><br> **TIME** <br> [ ] | | | | | | |
| TOTAL | | | | | | |

| | |
|---|---|
| **SNACKS** <br><br> **TIME** <br> [ ] | |

|  | CORE BODY | UPPER BODY | LOWER BODY |
|---|---|---|---|
| EXERCISES |  |  |  |
| SETS |  |  |  |
| REPS |  |  |  |
| WEIGHTS |  |  |  |
| REST TIME |  |  |  |

|  | WARM UP | COOL DOWN |
|---|---|---|
| ACTIVITY |  |  |
| SETS |  |  |
| REPS |  |  |
| TIME |  |  |
| DIST |  |  |
| INTENSITY |  |  |

GOALS: _____

_____

_____

_____

_____

_____

_____

_____

_____

DAY: _____

NAME: _____

| | DESCRIPTION | QTY | PROTEINS | VEGGIES | FRUITS & NUTS | FATS |
|---|---|---|---|---|---|---|
| **BREAKFAST**<br><br>TIME<br>⬚ | | | | | | |
| | | | | | | |
| | | | | | | |
| | | | | | | |
| TOTAL | | | | | | |

| | | | | | | |
|---|---|---|---|---|---|---|
| **LUNCH**<br><br>TIME<br>⬚ | | | | | | |
| | | | | | | |
| | | | | | | |
| | | | | | | |
| TOTAL | | | | | | |

| | | | | | | |
|---|---|---|---|---|---|---|
| **DINNER**<br><br>TIME<br>⬚ | | | | | | |
| | | | | | | |
| | | | | | | |
| | | | | | | |
| TOTAL | | | | | | |

| | |
|---|---|
| **SNACKS**<br><br>TIME<br>⬚ | |

|  | CORE BODY | UPPER BODY | LOWER BODY |
|---|---|---|---|
| EXERCISES | | | |
| SETS | | | |
| REPS | | | |
| WEIGHTS | | | |
| REST TIME | | | |

|  | WARM UP | COOL DOWN |
|---|---|---|
| ACTIVITY | | |
| SETS | | |
| REPS | | |
| TIME | | |
| DIST | | |
| INTENSITY | | |

GOALS: _____

_____

_____

_____

_____

_____

_____

_____

_____

DAY: _____

NAME: _____

| | DESCRIPTION | QTY | PROTEINS | VEGGIES | FRUITS & NUTS | FATS |
|---|---|---|---|---|---|---|
| **BREAKFAST**<br><br>**TIME** | | | | | | |
| **TOTAL** | | | | | | |

| | | | | | | |
|---|---|---|---|---|---|---|
| **LUNCH**<br><br>**TIME** | | | | | | |
| **TOTAL** | | | | | | |

| | | | | | | |
|---|---|---|---|---|---|---|
| **DINNER**<br><br>**TIME** | | | | | | |
| **TOTAL** | | | | | | |

| | |
|---|---|
| **SNACKS**<br><br>**TIME** | |

|  | CORE BODY | UPPER BODY | LOWER BODY |
|---|---|---|---|
| EXERCISES | | | |
| SETS | | | |
| REPS | | | |
| WEIGHTS | | | |
| REST TIME | | | |

|  | WARM UP | COOL DOWN |
|---|---|---|
| ACTIVITY | | |
| SETS | | |
| REPS | | |
| TIME | | |
| DIST | | |
| INTENSITY | | |

GOALS: _____

_____

_____

_____

_____

_____

_____

_____

DAY: _____

NAME: _____

| | DESCRIPTION | QTY | PROTEINS | VEGGIES | FRUITS & NUTS | FATS |
|---|---|---|---|---|---|---|
| **BREAKFAST** | | | | | | |
| | | | | | | |
| **TIME** | | | | | | |
| | | | | | | |
| **TOTAL** | | | | | | |

| | DESCRIPTION | QTY | PROTEINS | VEGGIES | FRUITS & NUTS | FATS |
|---|---|---|---|---|---|---|
| **LUNCH** | | | | | | |
| | | | | | | |
| **TIME** | | | | | | |
| | | | | | | |
| **TOTAL** | | | | | | |

| | DESCRIPTION | QTY | PROTEINS | VEGGIES | FRUITS & NUTS | FATS |
|---|---|---|---|---|---|---|
| **DINNER** | | | | | | |
| | | | | | | |
| **TIME** | | | | | | |
| | | | | | | |
| **TOTAL** | | | | | | |

| | |
|---|---|
| **SNACKS** | |
| | |
| **TIME** | |
| | |

|  | CORE BODY | UPPER BODY | LOWER BODY |
|---|---|---|---|
| EXERCISES |  |  |  |
| SETS |  |  |  |
| REPS |  |  |  |
| WEIGHTS |  |  |  |
| REST TIME |  |  |  |

|  | WARM UP | COOL DOWN |
|---|---|---|
| ACTIVITY |  |  |
| SETS |  |  |
| REPS |  |  |
| TIME |  |  |
| DIST |  |  |
| INTENSITY |  |  |

GOALS: _____

_____

_____

_____

_____

_____

_____

_____

_____

DAY: _____

NAME: _____

| | DESCRIPTION | QTY | PROTEINS | VEGGIES | FRUITS & NUTS | FATS |
|---|---|---|---|---|---|---|
| **BREAKFAST** | | | | | | |
| | | | | | | |
| **TIME** | | | | | | |
| | | | | | | |
| **TOTAL** | | | | | | |

| | DESCRIPTION | QTY | PROTEINS | VEGGIES | FRUITS & NUTS | FATS |
|---|---|---|---|---|---|---|
| **LUNCH** | | | | | | |
| | | | | | | |
| **TIME** | | | | | | |
| | | | | | | |
| **TOTAL** | | | | | | |

| | DESCRIPTION | QTY | PROTEINS | VEGGIES | FRUITS & NUTS | FATS |
|---|---|---|---|---|---|---|
| **DINNER** | | | | | | |
| | | | | | | |
| **TIME** | | | | | | |
| | | | | | | |
| **TOTAL** | | | | | | |

| | |
|---|---|
| **SNACKS** | |
| **TIME** | |

|  | CORE BODY | UPPER BODY | LOWER BODY |
|---|---|---|---|
| EXERCISES |  |  |  |
| SETS |  |  |  |
| REPS |  |  |  |
| WEIGHTS |  |  |  |
| REST TIME |  |  |  |

|  | WARM UP | COOL DOWN |
|---|---|---|
| ACTIVITY |  |  |
| SETS |  |  |
| REPS |  |  |
| TIME |  |  |
| DIST |  |  |
| INTENSITY |  |  |

GOALS: _____

_____

_____

_____

_____

_____

_____

_____

_____

DAY: _____

NAME: _____

| | | DESCRIPTION | QTY | PROTEINS | VEGGIES | FRUITS & NUTS | FATS |
|---|---|---|---|---|---|---|---|
| **BREAKFAST** | | | | | | | |
| | | | | | | | |
| TIME | | | | | | | |
| | | | | | | | |
| TOTAL | | | | | | | |

| | | | | | | | |
|---|---|---|---|---|---|---|---|
| LUNCH | | | | | | | |
| | | | | | | | |
| TIME | | | | | | | |
| | | | | | | | |
| TOTAL | | | | | | | |

| | | | | | | | |
|---|---|---|---|---|---|---|---|
| DINNER | | | | | | | |
| | | | | | | | |
| TIME | | | | | | | |
| | | | | | | | |
| TOTAL | | | | | | | |

| | |
|---|---|
| SNACKS | |
| TIME | |

|  | CORE BODY | UPPER BODY | LOWER BODY |
|---|---|---|---|
| EXERCISES | | | |
| SETS | | | |
| REPS | | | |
| WEIGHTS | | | |
| REST TIME | | | |

|  | WARM UP | COOL DOWN |
|---|---|---|
| ACTIVITY | | |
| SETS | | |
| REPS | | |
| TIME | | |
| DIST | | |
| INTENSITY | | |

GOALS: _____

_____

_____

_____

_____

_____

_____

_____

_____

DAY: _____

NAME: _____

| | | DESCRIPTION | QTY | PROTEINS | VEGGIES | FRUITS & NUTS | FATS |
|---|---|---|---|---|---|---|---|
| **BREAKFAST** | | | | | | | |
| **TIME** | | | | | | | |
| **TOTAL** | | | | | | | |

| | | | | | | | |
|---|---|---|---|---|---|---|---|
| **LUNCH** | | | | | | | |
| **TIME** | | | | | | | |
| **TOTAL** | | | | | | | |

| | | | | | | | |
|---|---|---|---|---|---|---|---|
| **DINNER** | | | | | | | |
| **TIME** | | | | | | | |
| **TOTAL** | | | | | | | |

| | |
|---|---|
| **SNACKS** | |
| **TIME** | |

|              | CORE BODY | UPPER BODY | LOWER BODY |
|--------------|-----------|------------|------------|
| EXERCISES    |           |            |            |
| SETS         |           |            |            |
| REPS         |           |            |            |
| WEIGHTS      |           |            |            |
| REST TIME    |           |            |            |

|           | WARM UP | COOL DOWN |
|-----------|---------|-----------|
| ACTIVITY  |         |           |
| SETS      |         |           |
| REPS      |         |           |
| TIME      |         |           |
| DIST      |         |           |
| INTENSITY |         |           |

GOALS: _____

_____

_____

_____

_____

_____

_____

_____

_____